VEHICLES

TRUCKS

Written by Bethany Latham

Genius Kid

sales@northstareditions.com | 888-417-0195

Library of Congress Control Number:
2025943954

ISBN
979-8-89471-068-6 (library bound)
979-8-89471-088-4 (paperback)
979-8-89471-124-9 (epub)
979-8-89471-108-9 (hosted ebook)

Printed in the United States of America
Mankato, MN
012026

Written by:
Bethany Latham

Edited by:
Rebecca Phillips-Bartlett

Designed by:
Ker Ker Lee

Photo Credits – Images courtesy of Shutterstock.com, unless otherwise stated.

Cover – Vereshchagin Dmitry, irin-k, aappp, Mr.1, Natdanai99, Siwakorn1933, I'm friday, Another77, Semjonow Juri, UladzimirZuyeu, Cara Kate, brizmaker. 2–3 – Senohrabek, 5m3photos. 4–5 – Bragapictures, Maksim Safaniuk, Another77, Oporty786. 6–7 – Nikolai Tsvetkov, BigTunaOnline, Cobalt S-Elinoi, InFocus.ee. 8–9 – a_v_d, Dub Dub studio, Francesco Scatena, Natata, AKaiser, Morphart Creation. 10–11 – irin-k, algre, Another77, alexgo.photography. 12–13 – Adisa. 14–15 – DmytroPerov, JoshBryan, notsuperstar, Knot. P. Saengma. 16–17 – Matveev Aleksandr, Pannawish. 18–19 – rocharibeiro, Sanit Fuangnakhon, fast-stock, Ceri Breeze. 20–21 – Holger Kleine, Piu_Piu, Petr Student. 22–23 – Manbetta, MAOIKO, Nigel Jarvis, Gualberto Becerra, Sergey Spritnyuk, Sanit Fuangnakhon.

CONTENTS

Words that look like this can be found in the glossary on page 24.

TRUCKS

Do you ever see trucks on the road when you're driving?

Trucks are vehicles made to transport goods or items. They usually travel on roads. Many trucks have more wheels than other vehicles.

What types of truck can you think of?

Trucks come in different sizes. They are often very large and heavy. Trucks have many uses, such as transporting liquids or towing other vehicles.

Trucks help us in many ways. Can you imagine a world without garbage trucks or fire engines?

KEY WORDS

Here are some key words about trucks that every genius kid should learn.

CAB

The cab is the part of the truck the driver sits in.

CHASSIS

The chassis is the frame of the truck. It is what everything else is built on.

STRAIGHT TRUCK

On a straight truck, everything fits on the same chassis. Box trucks are a type of straight truck.

ARTICULATED TRUCK

An articulated truck is made of more than one part joined together. Semitrucks are a type of articulated truck.

DID YOU KNOW?

Truck comes from the ancient Greek word *trokhos*. *Trokhos* means "wheel."

A TIMELINE OF TRUCKS

Trucks have changed a lot over time.

Pre-Trucks
Before trucks, people used carts pulled by animals.

1769
Nicolas-Joseph Cugnot built a steam-powered vehicle to carry heavy objects.

The Mid-1800s
Most goods were transported by steam wagons.

1896
The first truck with a combustion engine was built by Gottlieb Daimler and Wilhelm Maybach.

The 1960s–1970s
In the United States, diesel-powered engines became the most common type of engine for trucks.

Now
The United States has more than 14 million trucks.

TYPES OF TRUCKS

There are many kinds of trucks. They are designed to do different things.

Tanker trucks carry large amounts of liquids or gases.

Tanker trucks

Semitrucks are also called 18-wheelers. They deliver goods such as food or clothes.

Semitruck

Dump trucks transport loose materials such as gravel or sand.

Dump truck

Flatbed trucks transport large or strangely shaped goods.

Flatbed truck

Garbage trucks collect trash.

Garbage truck

TRUCK PARTS

On the outside, many trucks have the same parts.

Side-view mirrors help drivers see the area behind their truck.

The tractor contains the engine and the driver's cab.

Lights help the driver see at night.

The cargo area is where goods are stored.

The truck's wheels are attached to the axle. Larger trucks have more axles.

Truck wheels are very strong to support the truck's weight.

IN THE DRIVER'S SEAT

On the inside, trucks have many parts that help them work.

The steering wheel controls the direction the truck drives.

The gearshift helps the driver change gears.

Steering wheel

DID YOU KNOW?

Because trucks are big and heavy, they often have more gears than other vehicles.

The dashboard tells the driver information about the truck, such as how fast it is going.

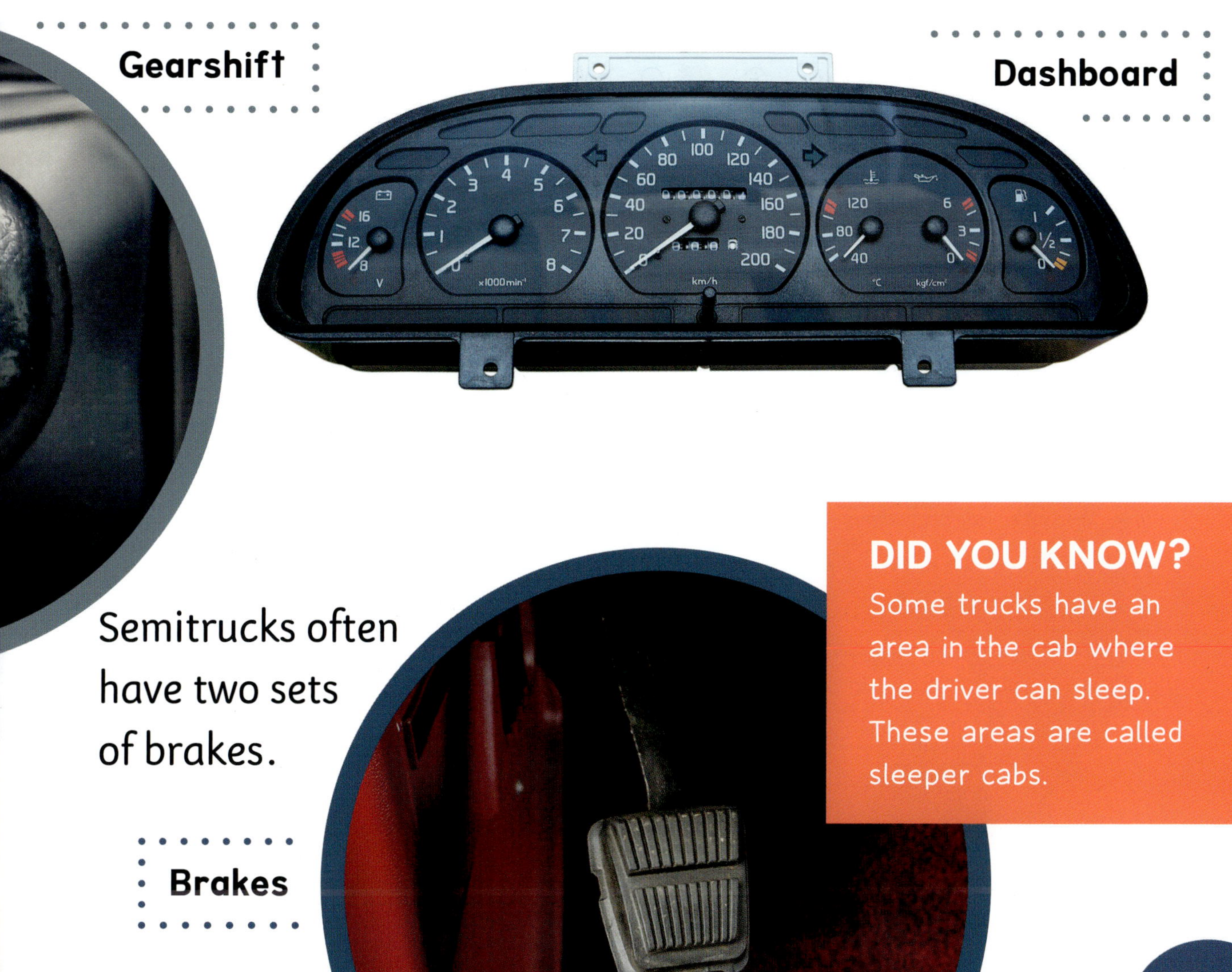

Semitrucks often have two sets of brakes.

DID YOU KNOW?
Some trucks have an area in the cab where the driver can sleep. These areas are called sleeper cabs.

INSIDE THE ENGINE

Most trucks have internal combustion engines. Truck engines usually use diesel as fuel. Diesel is a liquid made from oil.

In a diesel engine, air is pulled into the engine and squeezed. This makes the air heat up.

Then fuel is added to the air. The heat from the air ignites the fuel. This creates a small explosion.

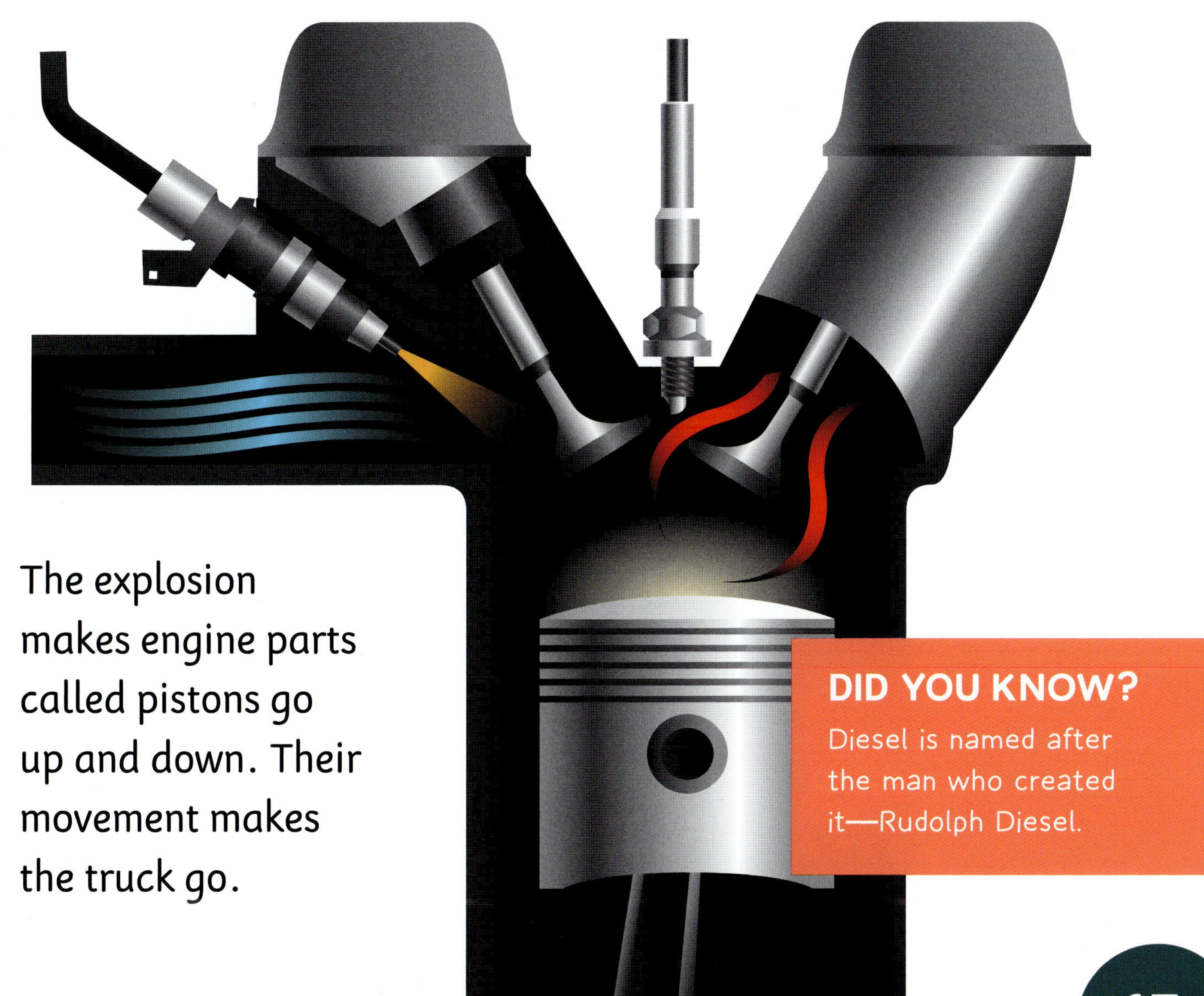

The explosion makes engine parts called pistons go up and down. Their movement makes the truck go.

DID YOU KNOW?

Diesel is named after the man who created it—Rudolph Diesel.

SAFETY FIRST

There are many things in a truck that keep the driver and passengers safe.

Brakes are very important in a truck. Trucks are heavy, so their brakes must be very strong.

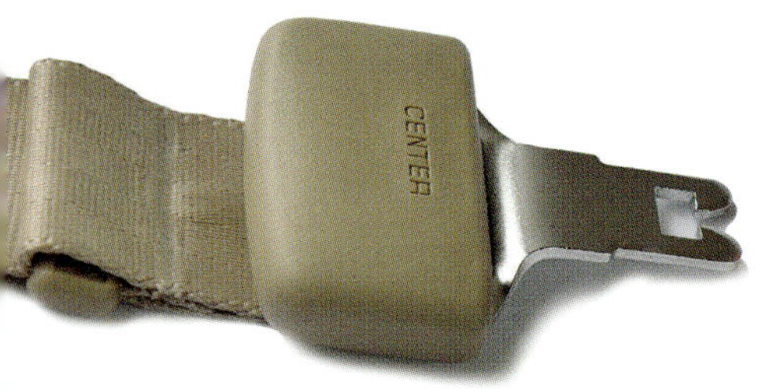

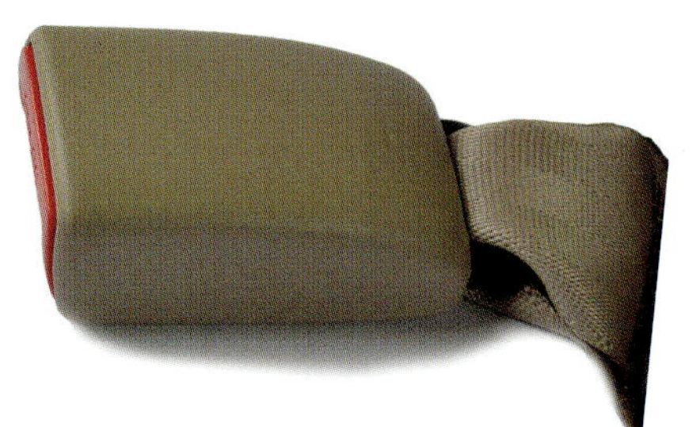

Seatbelts keep passengers safe in case of an accident.

Cameras and electronic sensors help the driver see outside the vehicle. They help the driver check the truck's blind spots.

A horn lets other people know the truck is there.

Safety signs on the truck tell other drivers to be careful when driving near it.

BELIEVE IT OR NOT!

In Australia, heavy goods are often transported by very large trucks called road trains. One tractor pulls many trailers.

Some trucks transport goods in very cold places. They travel over frozen rivers on roads made of ice.

In 2009, William Coe Jr. won a world record for driving the longest total distance in a commercial vehicle without a crash. He drove 3,001,276 miles (4,830,086 km).

Women began driving trucks during World War I.

ARE YOU A GENIUS KID?

Now you have many amazing truck facts to impress your friends and family with. But first, it is time to test your knowledge. Are you really a genius kid?

Check back through the book if you are not sure.

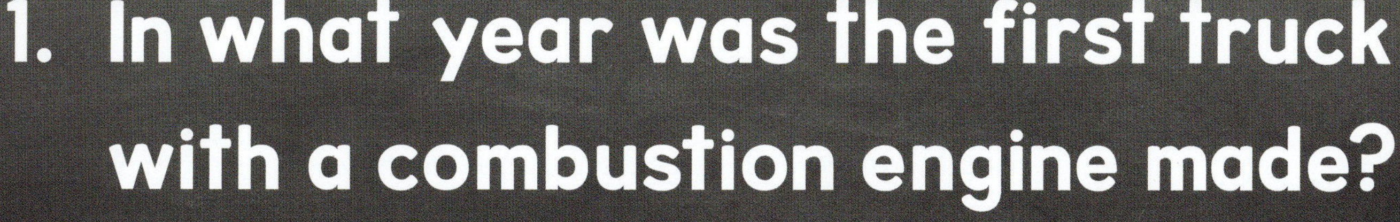

1. In what year was the first truck with a combustion engine made?
2. What is the name of a truck built to carry gravel and sand?
3. What type of fuel do most truck engines use?

Answers:
1. 1896
2. dump truck
3. diesel

GLOSSARY

blind spots areas around a vehicle that the driver cannot see

cargo goods carried on a large transport vehicle

combustion engine an engine that is powered by burning or setting fire to something

fuel something that can be used to make energy or power something

gears parts of a machine that make other parts move; different gears help trucks move at different speeds

ignites causes to catch fire or explode

vehicles machines that are used to carry people or things

INDEX